Words of a Starr.

J. Starr

BookLeaf Publishing

Presentation by *BookLeaf Publishing*

Web: www.bookleafpub.com

E-mail: info@bookleafpub.com

ISBN: 9789357692045

First edition 2022

DEDICATION

To my family and friends,

JOLO!

Without you all, this would not have been possible.

ACKNOWLEDGEMENT

I'd like to acknowledge my friends, and family who believed in me and motivated me to complete this challenge, when I was too afraid to believe in myself.

A special thanks to my creative editor in chief - Henry Young Shel.

The Mantra.

It's going to be ok.
It's going to be alright.
When in doubt remember,
THIS. AIN'T. IT.

Repeat until belief.

Seasons

The warmth of this October wind, drapes my
body and hugs it tightly
Like a blanket right out of the dryer
The trees have changed, lining the roadways
with the perfect hues of fall
22 degrees on the 22nd of October
Is it Spring?
Is it Fall?
The seasons seem to be as confused as I am
Yet just like the seasons
We continue to grow
and change
and fuse
into the different
seasons of life.

Sun-date

Disdain.
Distaste.
Displeased.

Diwali '22

Turn on all the lights.
Yes every single one.
Today we invite in light over darkness.
Today we celebrate our victories
Good over evil
Because for one single day, the darkness does
not have to win.

Today we embrace all the light forms available
to us
It's within the beams of the sun that I find
glimpses of hope.
The warmth of the sun,
So tangible as it penetrates layers of skin
Melting away the aches
She follows me every step of the way.
Sometimes lighting the path in front, sometimes
illuminating the path behind.

Today before we ignite the external flames of
our victories
Let us reach within and spark our inner flames
Let the light from within beam so warm and
bright;
That darkness and evil could not bare to stand
within the shadows of you

Game of Life

The calm before the storm
The warmth before the cold
Life doesn't seem to stop for anyone.
Heck not me for sure
It continues to chug along, day after day, minute
after minute with no regards for those who can't
keep up.
We have no choice but to waddle along,
crawl along,
not at any particular pace
but the one that is our own.
Life is not a sprint,
it's a marathon.
So buckle yourself up, because the race is far
from over
and in it we remain, the key players in this game
called life.

Brown Skinned

Why do they always say we came over here and
took their jobs?
If the job was theirs would they have not secured
it?
How could a brown skinned person waltz in and
take what you claim is yours?
How could the brown skin, beat you at what's
yours?
The audacity of the brown skin
To rise above and reach successes the pale did
not think possible.
How dare us.
How dare us?
How dare you?!
Unable to accept defeat handed down by brown
hands.
The humiliation you must feel, that our curry
laced skin, could out rank you.
Could out beat you.
How dare we rise above our successors and
challenge the status quo.
Shaping a future, where the brown skin, may be
the fairest of them all.

Identity

The complexities of our identities
We are all prisms of our experiences
Yet in prisoned to our experiences

Scent

Funny how a scent can send you time travelling,
To a far off memory.
A moment so clear,
So tangible, like you could have sworn you were there.
A fading scent, that lingers but vanishes like
water droplets evaporating into the air

Zoey

You glance back at me with your brown eyes
Whiskers curled up in a smirk
I wonder what naughty thought you have
You keep me guessing
On my toes as you run around on all four
We are one
You are me
And I am you
Together we roll through these streets
What is for you, ends up being for me
Those walks around the block, keep the mind at
ease
Together we roam, free.
I watch you sleep, ears flopped like Yoda
You are your own Yoda
You are my Yoda
The lessons you have taught
The lessons you still teach
I am grateful for your presence with me

Privilege

The privilege to never have to learn to live a life
you never chose for you.
The privilege in never having to mourn the life
you had,
From the trenches of the new life you're being
forced to create.
The privilege to not have any choice
But to embrace the unknown
Because that is the only known.
The privilege you hold, is the privilege you took
away from me.

Lingering Lover

Today you finally leave
Today we say our final goodbyes
We said them years ago but you've lingered ever since
Faintly behind the scenes but never too far from recall
The love that I received,
The lessons I learned at your hands,
The entirety of me will forever be grateful.
To have experienced something so rare,
So beautiful,
So soft and nurturing,
Oh what I will do to keep that experience alive
But that experience cannot consume me anymore.
It cannot be the only experience defining my life.
What lays behind the door has to be be better than what has no more life.
Not more active energy fuelling the embers of our connection.
Smouldering the flame,
I walk forward with anticipation for what happens next.

Rexdale

This is to Rexdale
To the streets that raised me
The opportunities and doors that opened for me
As I walked down these streets,
I see what a privilege it is,
To bare the colour of my skin.
I bow down to the days of adversity,
That humbled me, and taught me how to
persevere
There, here, and anywhere.

Nothing was the same

Nothing was the same,
After that hit
After that drop
After that dishonesty

But nothing was supposed to stay the same.
Isn't that the way the world works?
The irony.

"The lack of effort got us looking different."
Yeah, got us searching and revealing That
you've been cheating while I've been healing.

"What more can I say now?"

The force of your clenched fist hitting the back
of my head, it still aches - echos. Yet the
softness of your lips,
The gentleness of your love,
The lessons you taught me,
Still guide me.
I might be "the furthest thing from perfect"
But I am strong.

March 20, 2020

I don't want to be here anymore.
I am empty.
Alone.
Invisible.
A no one.
I want to be out of my misery.
I don't have a place anywhere.
Excluded.
Isolated.
I'm an inconvenience.
Take this pain from me and release me.
Just let me go.

#More

Better is all I want
To be better.
To demand better.
To do better.
To continue growing and actively accepting all
that comes into my path.
It's a scary thought because to want and expect
better from yourself
And in return others,
Requires such self exposure and is the ultimate
form of vulnerability,
And that's intimidating.
I can't help but ask,
Am I there?
Am I ready to let myself be that exposed?
Will I ever be ready?
How will I know when the right time is,
If I don't know what the right time is for?
Am I walking blindly,
Or am I not accepting the truth
Which lies down this path I choose not to see?
Alone?
Is that possible?
Can my love alone lead this path?
Is my love large enough?

If it isn't, don't I want my self-love to be large
enough to light the way for me?
If so, then why aren't I working towards that?
What am I waiting for?
It starts with me, and not them.
Me.
Be better,
Do better,
And better will come.

Specks

"It's all the things you can't explain" ..

.. the push and the pull; the way this world
works is beyond my understanding.
Bringing together strangers to form the most
important bonds of our lives, with people that
we'll come to call family.
Then one day, after countless years together, we
have to just let go?
Blindsided by this part of life, who can say that
this is even remotely close to fair?
And now she cries because no one can prevent
what's yet to come.
That's her heart and soul, her reason.
And she is my reason, so what happens when
she begins to crumble?
It's a chain reaction waiting to be set off and I
can't bear to see anyone hurt .. especially her.
Hang onto my words – we will see this through.
Hope; tighten your grip around it and don't let it
go because it's all we have left.
Black spots or not, this isn't the end
Believe that.
And if by chance this is the end, then our world
will be hit by an enormous disaster

A great, wise man will be lost.
But lost doesn't mean forgotten and lost also
doesn't mean gone,
but it doesn't mean here either.
Being at a loss for words is where comfort
seems to lurk
Hearing your voice is hard but know that not
speaking right now doesn't mean that we love
you any less, but that ..
"It's only fear that runs through my veins. It's all
the things you can't explain, that make us
human"

R.I.P. Nana

~ May 17, 2011

Addiction

You swore you'd never do it again
Yet you did
7 years later and you turned to the same bottle
that turned against you
You took the same shot that let you down time
after time
And what'd it heal?
Nothing.
That voice, oh the voice
Anyone could recognize it from a mile away
It's the demon in you speaking, the alcohol
By now you're thoughts aren't evening flowing
Your walk is crossed
And your head is spinning
You get up to express your feelings but you
stumble.
You fall down.
You swore you were stronger than this but the
bottle proved to be stronger
When shit got rough, you turned to a gin on the
rocks
You were stronger than this
You lasted 7 years but now you're back where
you started
In a grave dug 6 feet too deep

The demon inside you, was my nightmare
My fear
But that demon no longer haunts me
Slurred words and drunken rages are the
essences behind my solid exteriorMeanwhile
your interior is filled with liquid poison
That takes away precious seconds from your life
From the beautiful person I know you are
But your addiction drowns you
And you fade away
You say you don't know what's wrong but the
answer to your problems is clear.You're an
addict and you could never be considered
anything else.
Yet, somewhere, somehow, I still love you.

~ January 5th, 2010

Attachment Theory

The attachment is real
To a moment
To an experience
To the tangible souvenirs of your being.
I am intertwined within every fibre of my
memory
Held hostage by flashbacks
The daydreams that no longer remain
Replaced with a bleak reality
That, the attachment is real

Rage

Colours of red,
Colours of black
Darkness stares back at me
While my eyes burn of rage
There is no off switch
No kill switch
Only killing is of my soul that burns deep within
this rage
Yet again at the mercy of these emotions
Bring me down to my knees why don't you
Immobilize me and this feeling that is roaring
within

BC

BC,
You used to be my favourite province
Now you're just the initials of my dearly
departed.

R.I.P. my angels above
Bibi & Chacha

Home

I used to think home was a place
A location
I used to think home was a feeling
A person
I realize now
That home is wherever I am
I am home.